1 2 3 4 5 6 7 8 9 0

Absolutely
Mental

1

Also by Rowland Morgan

Absolutely Mental 2

Number Crunchers: Brain Bafflers

1 2 3 4 5 6 7 8 9 0

Absolutely
Mental
1

Rowland Morgan

Illustrated by
Mike Phillips

MACMILLAN CHILDREN'S BOOKS

First published 2000
by Macmillan Children's Books
a division of Macmillan Publishers Ltd
25 Eccleston Place, London SW1W 9NF
Basingstoke and Oxford
www.macmillan.co.uk

Associated companies throughout the world

ISBN 0 330 48172 X

1 3 5 7 9 8 6 4 2

A CIP catalogue record for this book is available from the British Library.

Printed by Mackays of Chatham plc, Chatham, Kent.

1 2 3 4 5 6 7 8 9 0

Contents

1 2 3 4 5 6 7 8 9 0

Absolutely Mental:
Introduction

In prehistoric times, before writing was invented, people demonstrated amazing mental power. Bards, for example, recited history from memory. In India, certain sacred scriptures, known as the Hindu Vedas, were about three times as long as the Holy Bible, but they were handed down from person to person by memory. This kind of mental recording lasted for many thousands of years. And the same applied to numbers. Numbers were spoken for hundreds of thousands of years before they were written down.

However, something strange happened when people finally thought of writing numbers down. For some reason, they immediately wanted help. Almost as soon as humans started to write down numbers, they invented crutches to support their brains. On the next page is a time-line of arithmetical brain-crutches:

1 2 3 4 5 6 7 8 9 0

Brain Crutches:
A time-line

30000 BC Notches on bones, etc
5000 BC Bamboo tallies or chips – used by, for example, the Chinese
4500 BC Calendars – invented by, for example, the Egyptians
3500 BC Quipu – beads on strings, best-known among the Aztecs
1000 BC Bead frame or abacus – from ancient Greece, ancient Rome & China
1600 AD Quadrant & theodolite – used for navigation by Europeans
1700 AD Logarithm tables – written by, amongst others, Isaac Newton of England
1800 AD Mechanical calculator – built by Charles Babbage of England
1850 AD Analytical engine – also by Babbage
1950 AD Electronic computer – made by Eckert & Mauchly in the USA
1963 AD Electronic calculator – made by Bell Punch Company USA
1979 AD Mini-computer – invented by Sir Clive Sinclair in Britain
1984 AD Apple Macintosh – one of its inventors, Steve Jobs, was just nineteen years old.

The first pocket calculators, produced in Cambridge by Clive Sinclair in 1972, cost about a week's wages. Twenty years later, one could be found in every child's school bag.

Then, wham!

After 30,000 years, someone important decided that brain-crutches for arithmetic had gone too far. Probably, it was because they had finally reached children in school. Anyway, it was announced that children had to start THINKING again. Instead of tapping two-times-two into their calculators and getting the answer "four" on the screen, they had to go "Um, two times two, that's um, er, um, FIVE." The funny thing is that brain-crutches have never been much use in a crisis. When Eve handed Adam an apple, he did not whip out a tally-stick to notch it up. He made a mental calculation: "One apple. Hmmm. Can't do much harm."

When Albert Einstein filled the 150th chalkboard with equations, he did not rush over to a mechanical computer the size of a factory; instead he did a few sums in his head and said: "Hey! I get it! Ee equals em cee squared!"

Numbers have always been magical, and there's a spark of genius in all of us when we figure things out on the spot. That's what these stories are all about – sparks of genius ... so let's get cracking!

rowland@splong.com

1 2 3 4 5 6 7 8 9 0

Almost a Million

Gerald Sikorsky felt drops of cold sweat bulging out of his forehead. The sound of his CD faded away. The sweat drops trickled down into his eyebrows. He blinked, losing for a fraction of a second his view of the screen. On it was an e-mail from his robot stockbroker at go-for-broker.com. The message was simple and shattering:

Dear Mr Sikorsky
Your shares in ka-ploing.com have increased from 07 cents to 746 dollars. Your 1000 shares are now worth $746,000. However, due to a securities commission inquiry, you can not sell them later than @499 (internet time).

"Internet time?" freaked Gerald, tearing his hair, and frantically keying the words into a return message. "What the heck is that?"
The robot replied annoyingly:

Internet Time represents a completely new global concept of time. Basically, the beat, the revolutionary new unit of time, means the following: No time zones. No geographical borders.
How long is a beat? Internet users have divided up the virtual and real day into 1000 beats. One beat is the

11

equivalent of 1 minute 26.4 seconds. That means that 12 noon in the old time system is the equivalent of @500 beats.

Internet Time is the same all over the world. How is this possible? A watchmaker has created a new meridian in Biel, Switzerland. Biel Mean Time (BMT) will be the universal reference for Internet Time. A day in Internet Time begins at midnight BMT Central European Wintertime – @000 beats. So it is the same time all over the world, be it night or day. The era of time zones has disappeared.

Gerald could see instantly that this was a clever idea, but he had never heard of it and now had no idea what time it was! It could cost him the best part of one million dollars! He could lose the chance to be the richest 12 year-old in his entire neighbourhood! He cursed the robot stockbroker and stared at his watch in a panic. It said: 11.57a.m.

Gerald goggled at the message. A beat was 1 minute and 26.4 seconds. So he figured that he had to divide the minutes since midnight by one point two-six-four.

He started scribbling desperately on his notepad.

Did Gerald get to be the richest 12 year-old on the block?

1 2 3 4 5 6 7 8 9 0

A Big Pile of Computer Games

Vlanski, the world-famous concert pianist, stood before his son, Fangio.

"Fangio, you're playing an 88-key concert grand piano that cost me a bundle."

"Yes, Father," said Fangio, who had learnt always to say yes to the great man.

"You have been taking lessons on it for two years, and you still have no idea how to play the scale of C, even with one hand. It is 5 June today. You return to boarding school on 1 September."

"Yes, Father," said Fangio.

"In order to persuade you to learn the piano, I am going to propose something," Vlanski said.

"Yes, Father," said Fangio.

"The only activity that excites you is computer games, so I am going to give you one for every note on the piano. I will buy them all when you have practised one day for every musical key this holiday, starting tomorrow. At school you will be able to show your teacher your excellent piano-playing, and your friends your stack of games. Do you agree?"

There was a brief silence.

"No, Father," said Fangio.

Why did Fangio, who always said yes, say no?

1 2 3 4 5 6 7 8 9 0

Block Head

The Astrojet Project was a square block of 36 white laboratory buildings arranged on a grid pattern of streets. None of the buildings were identified in any way. The whole complex was surrounded by high barbed wire. Cameras scanned every inch of it. Laser beams blocked any satellite view. Transmitters jammed all radar. Located in the middle of the Wabj desert in deepest Arabia, no roads led to it. There was only a heli-pad, defended by guided missiles. Beside the main gate, standing apart from the vast complex of laboratories, was a reception building.

In the main hall, Shamus Blond, Her Majesty's Special Agent Number 005, shook hands with Doctor Ezekiel Wrench, billionaire inventor of the Reverse Twinch Turbine. Wrench was the scheming mastermind behind the Astrojet Project which planned to build a human city on Neptune.

"We are delighted to see you, Mr Blond," said Doctor Wrench.

"I am delighted to be working for Her Majesty's government," Blond said, following the script he had learnt at HQ in the previous few days. "I wonder who you work for," he thought to himself.

Doctor Wrench gestured to the group of soberly dressed visitors to be quiet. "Our demonstration hall is in Lab One," he announced. "Obviously certain elements are top secret, but we are happy for the world to know the basic facts about what we are doing. We will be glad to answer your questions. Let me show you the way."

The main street cut the block of laboratories in half. The demonstration hall was in the first building on the right. Doctor Wrench and his staff explained the mission and its technology for two hours.

Afterwards, Blond found himself facing Doctor Wrench. The scientist spoke confidentially in a low voice. "I have arranged a special briefing for you and a few other senior officials from world bodies. We will gather in a secure building elsewhere," he said, stroking his bushy black beard.

"I am privileged," Blond replied, narrowing his eyes, wondering where the others were.

"First, I have to see off the main group of visitors," said the scientist. "We will meet in 15 minutes. This is the north side of the complex. Take the main street and go three blocks south. Turn right and go five blocks west. Enter the building on your right. Until then, goodbye."

Blond went immediately to his helicopter and ordered the pilot to leave the country.

Why?

1 2 3 4 5 6 7 8 9 0
Brave Knight

Lord Randall chuckled at the assembled knights. All of them were wearing their armour, ready for jousting. Only their visors were raised, revealing their war-like eyes. Behind them, a tournament was under way. Two knights pounded towards each other on armoured horses, their lances aimed. The Black Knight's lance was around 5 cm lower. Casually, the assembly of knights turned to watch the Black Knight getting toppled, and then they fixed their grim gazes back on Lord Randall. "Ha! What care I if King Henry has accepted my challenge?" he blustered. "I shall topple him easily."

"His Majesty is enormous," muttered Sir Toby Hildreth. "He sits 1 metre high in the saddle. Thou art a squirt, and sittest a mere 85 cm beside thy sovereign."

"Worry not," jeered Lord Randall, "my steed stands 18 hands high."(1)

"I wonder," murmured Sir Toby, "would it be wise to topple thy monarch?"

"King Henry is a sport," Lord Randall snorted.

By the royal marquee, grooms were readying the king for the joust.

"Lord Randall has sworn to topple you, your Majesty," one of them blurted, with a toothless grin.

"I've heard a bit about him," the King said, smiling. "To give the lad a fair chance, I shall ride Mountjoy, he stands only 17 hands high."

The watching courtiers applauded. The grooms nodded approvingly.

Why?

(1) Hand = 10 cm

1 2 3 4 5 6 7 8 9 0

Cake

"Cake is different from cakes," Dimple Ray liked to say when they asked him.

"Speaking as the heaviest man in the world and champion cake-eater," the reporters would ask, "what is your word on cake?"

"Cakes is one thing," he would slobber, wiping his mouth. "Cake is another."

They always frowned and asked him to explain.

"Cake is eaten in pieces," Dimple would say. "Cakes come in ones." The reporters would nod, pretending to understand. Few really did, though. They didn't realize that Dimple had learnt his lesson. It was one of the few things he knew. All that mountain of flesh and blubber that swelled up beneath his head had just about crushed his brains. There wasn't much room left for thought – he just ate. But at his very first cake-eating championship, years ago, Dimple Ray had been tricked.

"Tell ya what," said one of the champions he met at the contest. "Let's have a little challenge on the side. Most cakes wins."

Dimple Ray was already pretty full from the early knock-out rounds, but, heck, he loved to eat cake. He said, "yup."

The champion brought out a tray of assorted cakes: lots of little ones and a couple of really big ones, the size of bed pillows. A crowd gathered to watch.

Now Dimple Ray knew how to eat cake. He reckoned he could show everyone a thing or two. So, at the word "go", he grabbed up the biggest cake of all, a real monster he could hardly lift, and started to stuff it all into his mouth. He had to shove and twist and poke to get it all in. He was swallowing huge lumps as he pushed, but it still took a few minutes to ram it all down his throat.

His challenger popped a few little iced cupcakes into one cheek and munched, grinning at Dimple Ray's struggle with the enormous cake. When it had all gone down, he pronounced: "I win."

Dimple Ray's eyes bulged. "Hey, wait a minute," he slobbered. "I ate a cake the size of a bucket."

He appealed to the crowd.

What did they say?

1 2 3 4 5 6 7 8 9 0

Compass Conundrum

Captain Kneebone stared out of the window of the bridge, trying to establish whether the lenses of his binoculars were hazing over, or his brain. It had been an excellent lunch of tomato soup, chicken nuggets, chips and baked beans, and chocolate cake with custard. He had taken second helpings of each, and followed it all with two cups of strong hot chocolate. Now he could barely stand up and his ship's rudder control had failed, putting her in desperate danger.

The *MV Emblem Castle* was the flagship of the enormous Emblem oil company, and as such, was the largest oil-carrying supertanker in history. She weighed nearly half a million tonnes. Her payload of 150,000 tonnes of crude oil was worth a fortune, and could pollute an area of sea the size of England. At her normal cruising speed of 25 kilometres per hour, she could stop in five kilometres. Inside that distance, anything in her way got hit by the weight of 70 Eiffel Towers and utterly destroyed.

Drifting towards her, so to speak, at this moment, was the rocky coast of Mexico. If the *Emblem Castle* struck the coast, most of the sea of Cortez would be covered with a layer of poisonous crude oil. Tugs would never reach the scene in time. The sea of Cortez is one of the richest fishing areas left on earth. It is also home to many of the world's whales and dolphins.

Something seemed to have gone wrong with the ship's steering mechanism. She did not respond to any command from the helm. A moment earlier, the navigating officer had called out to Captain Kneebone, "Speed 25 kilometres per hour sir. Radar indicates the Mexican coast is four kilometres away. What are your orders?"

Kneebone struggled to make his brain work. He could not face the humiliation of asking his officers for help. If she's doing 25 kilometres per hour, he thought, through a fog of indigestion and nausea, she'll do four kilometres in, let's see, fours into sixty, take away 25, divided by – oh dear!

"Stand by!" he commanded sternly, his mind in a turmoil.

What happened?

Crag-Hanger

While mountain-climbing, Tara had an unexpected fall, and ended up dangling from a crag's edge by her fingertips.

Her friend Naomi screamed and tried to grab her hands. But she only succeeded in loosening them. Tara began to slip away, but, by a miracle, Naomi's fingertips suddenly hooked under hers.

Naomi spoke through gritted teeth, "Tony's uncoiling the rescue line, it'll only take seven seconds. Don't worry, we know that from hours of training."

One finger slipped loose. Tara counted as the others slipped out of Naomi's grip: "One-alligator, two-alligators, three-alligators," and started to pray.

Why?

1 2 3 4 5 6 7 8 9 0

Desert Dilemma

Ahmed pulled back the hood of his cloak and wiped the sweat from his brow. It was madness to travel across the Sahara desert by day, but his wife, Nizwara, had been kidnapped at dawn and taken to an oasis, seven days' journey away. There was no time to lose.

The trouble was, his hot-headed son, Nazreem, who had been to school in Timbuktu, was demanding that he call off the journey and offer the kidnappers a ransom through tribal channels instead.

"But it will take so much longer, possibly months," Ahmed had replied, staring at the dunes on the horizon, yearning to see the beautiful Nizwara again. "And who knows what might happen to her in the meantime."

Nazreem stared at his father: a great man, but a stubborn, impulsive one, who was about to make his biggest mistake – one which could cost the family all its best camels. They would be ruined and he, Nazreem, would lose his inheritance and become the laughing stock of the village.

"Esteemed father, listen to reason," he said. "Each camel drinks about 200 litres of water at a time." He gestured at the animals, which were at that moment dipping their long necks to draw water at the oasis. "1 litre will keep a camel going for about one hour. Work it out for yourself – your camels will be dead long before we reach Nizwara. We will be left to die of exposure in the desert. You will be a laughing stock and I will be ridiculed for the rest of my life."

Ahmed studied his son: a fine boy, but stubborn, impulsive.

He turned to his groom and said, "Saddle up the camels."

Why?

Detective Doubt

Detective Ray Ruggles stared worriedly up and down the row of suspects ranged before him at the vicarage. His boss, Chief Detective Wobble, examined him with a beady eye. Ruggles tried not to blush, feeling the hard stare of the chief drilling into him.

"One more blunder, Ruggles, and you're out," Wobble had said only a few days before, standing there behind his desk at the station, staring down at his junior officer as if he were nothing more than a worm. "We can't have officers on the Parkville force acting like fools in public. We'll become a laughing stock, and order will break down. If you're caught acting the dimwit just once more, you'll be looking for a job cleaning toilets, or de-worming mice."

Ruggles winced, remembering the scene, and stared at the vicar's daughter. Had she had an alibi? He could see the docket in his mind's eye: four of the five had good alibis, three women and one man. They could not have committed the murder. But the docket had been filed last week. He was supposed to remember, but he couldn't, for the life of him.

Scratching his head, he turned to look at the two maids, the upstairs maid and the kitchen maid. Which of them had poisoned the vicar? He had no idea.

"Ahem!" said the Chief, loudly indicating that he expected Ruggles to accuse the guilty party.

Ruggles stared wildly at the gardener and the lad, his apprentice, almost pointed at one of them, but, at the last moment, swung his finger round to point at the vicar's daughter.

"Miss Whistle, I accuse you of murdering your father. Please come with us to the station at once."

Did Ruggles keep his job?

Disc Dilemma

Clara Clay faced the board of directors in the high-rise offices of the world's biggest record company. She was being interviewed for the top job: Head of Global Sales.

The chairman leaned forward across the oak table. His steely eyes bored into hers. He was one of the richest men in the world, and one of the cleverest.

"Here's the offer," he snapped, "and it's a generous one. We pay you enough per month to buy a stack of compact discs as tall as you are. No other record company will ever match that. Take it or leave it."

Clara held the chairman's gaze. She was one metre eighty tall, and she rapidly worked out that enough 1mm-thick compact discs to stack as high as the top of her head could be a superb deal. But she knew that the chairman had a devious mind. She turned down the offer and walked out.

Why?

1 2 3 4 5 6 7 8 9 0

DJ Sonic

DJ Sonic purred into the microphone at rock station Crack-
a-rack. He glanced up at the clock on the studio wall.
11.28 pm. Spot-on!

"Now, folks, this new CD single by Shala Twangle is
groovy in every way. First, it's the most humungous sound
invented. Second, it's a majorly cool song, two minutes of
sheer music heaven. Third, there are four takes of it on this
disc. You couldn't ask for more. Now I'm going to take you
up to my midnight sign-off by playing these four versions in
every different order possible. Get that? No way you can
ever hear these four funky versions in any other sequence.
Sixteen different ways, that's 32 minutes of rockin' paradise.
You betcha."

Johnny, the engineer, started waving from behind the soundproof glass of the control room. DJ Sonic took no notice.

"I have a random-order button here in front of me that makes this possible automatically. You are really going to dig this experience."

Johnny tapped on the window, but it did no good.

"Yeah, it's a long session of Shala Twangle, but there's not one rock fan in this country who'd turn it down."

Johnny tore off his headset and banged it against the window.

"So, here goes, friends. Dig it!" DJ Sonic flipped the toggle switch on his control panel and smiled as the first bars of Shala Twangle's Number One hit blasted out.

Johnny burst into the studio. "Hey, Sonic, we'll be getting calls all night. You blew it."

What did Johnny mean?

Electro-Detector

In the 1950s, the government introduced the TV detector van. It could detect a TV working in a house, even if the owner had hidden the aerial in the attic to avoid paying a TV licence.

In 2008, governments across the world introduced the electro-detector van. It could detect electricity consumption exceeding 2,000 watts in any house. This limit had been imposed to help stop global warming, which was destroying the Earth's climate.

The electro-detector vans cruised round at night (using solar power collected by day), checking out people's power consumption. Of course, they were no more popular than the TV detector vans had been in their day. Soon, shops started selling electro-detector detectors.

People with "intelligent" houses programmed the house to turn things off when the alarm went. It worked automatically. If the electro-detector van came near, the intelligent house reduced its electricity consumption to fewer than 2,000 watts with a single click.

In older houses, people fitted them under the stairs, or in the kitchen cupboard, and waited for the alarm to go off. Then they raced round the house turning things off. They turned off computers, heaters, TVs, stereos, irons, washing machines, cookers, radios, electric blankets, make-up mirrors, hairdryers — you name it, they turned it off.

Jamie Barr's family was not well enough off to have an intelligent house. In fact, their house was pretty unintelligent. It was a ramshackle old place with poor insulation and it required plenty of electric heating. It had rambling corridors, twisting stairs, an attic, a cellar, and lots of small rooms, each heated by an individual 750-watt electric heater, that had to be turned on or off.

Jamie's dad had bought an electro-detector detector. When the alarm went off, Jamie's dad started shouting, because there was a stiff fine for using more than 2,000 watts. Jamie had to turn off everything in his bedroom except the fish-tank. Its light and pump used only 25 watts, and he was allowed not to upset the fish. On the other hand, he had to make sure his TV was not left on standby, because it used 17 watts that were wasted.

In 2009, a meeting of world leaders decided that not enough was being done. The electro-detector fine was doubled.

Not long after, on a chilly winter evening, Jamie's mum and dad went out to a meeting. They told Jamie's babysitter Mary that, in case the electro-detector detector alarm went off, they were leaving equipment on that used only 1,800

33

watts. She had to check that Jamie's bedroom did not take the total over 2,000.

At 8.35 the alarm went off. Jamie had persuaded Mary not to make him go to bed, so he was with her when she checked his warm, cosy bedroom. The TV was on standby, so she turned it off. The fish-tank was on, but she did not like fish, so she turned it off. The main light in the room was 100 watts, so she turned it off. Jamie's reading light was 60 watts. She left it on and made him get into bed with his book. She looked round the room and noticed a red light on his mobile phone. It was charging. She disconnected it from the mains. After another look round, she said goodnight and went downstairs to watch the TV.

Jamie lay in bed, thinking, "Well, we checked carefully. I hope Dad doesn't get that double fine."

Did he?

1234567890

Expedition

Sir Algernon Fortescue, professor of Deserts at Stoneford University, recently led the first successful crossing of the Nabi desert.

At a dinner held in his honour at the Royal Desert Exploration Society in Stoneford, Sir Algernon gave a talk. It caused a storm of interest; yet another to add to a colourful and adventurous career.

The explorer revealed for the first time how narrowly he and his party had escaped death on their perilous journey across the vast interior of Arabia. Here are some excerpts from his speech:

"We knew that we would be facing extremes of temperature as we travelled on our route due north – blazing heat by day, freezing cold by night. After considerable thought, study and reflection, I came up with an idea. We should take food. I am proud to say that the rest of the team immediately approved this suggestion. During training, the question came up: what kind of food should we be taking with us? Fortunately, being a professor puts me in touch with many great minds at the cutting edge of their various fields of knowledge. I wrote to the Regius Professor of Cake in the department of Cake Studies. In my letter I asked his advice about food in the desert. The reply came back by return of post. 'Cake,' he suggested. And so cake it was.

"My cook provided an excellent round fruit cake, and my assistant cut it in half. He then cut each half in half. You will immediately understand that this procedure yielded four equal pieces.

"We travelled for many days. We ate three quarter-pieces of cake. Eventually we noticed a rock that we recognized. It became clear that we were going in circles. We were, in a word, lost. Fortunately, when the sun rose next morning, using the remaining piece of cake, I was able to guide us out of the desert. The rest is history."

How did the Professor perform this feat?

1 2 3 4 5 6 7 8 9 0

Farran's Frightener

Farran's was the smartest bakery in the smartest district of the smartest borough of London. It sold smartly designed cakes and pastries to some of the most smartly dressed people in Europe.

On Tuesday, November 23rd, 20—, scandal struck. The police arrived and shut down the shop, arresting Mr and Mrs Farran and their son Sultan. Thirty-six very smart people had suddenly dropped dead in their smart townhouses, and fresh Farran's paper bags, smelling of apple danish, had been found near each of the bodies.

The four remaining specimens of Farran's popular apple danish were removed from the shop in evidence bags, and conveyed to the Metropolitan Police forensic laboratory for urgent tests. To the grim satisfaction of police officers, all four £1 apple danishes were found to contain trace elements of epithalium monoxydisulphide, a very rare poison, very occasionally found in certain strains of imported flour. One average-sized human being had to consume at least three of the tainted apple danishes in order to die suddenly, it was stated. No guilt was attached to the Farrans, and the police were obliged to release them. Nevertheless, the bakery's reputation was ruined and something had to be done to restore it.

On returning from the police station, Sultan immediately studied the bakery accounts. The shop till roll did not identify what items had been sold, so it was difficult to tell how many of the six dozen apple danishes had been bought. Only one other item, the chocolate eclair, sold for exactly £1. A total of 146 purchases had been made, adding up to £563. Sultan hurriedly called the local newspaper. An article was published, and the shop was completely exonerated.

How?

1 2 3 4 5 6 7 8 9 0

Fatal Food

The Empress Mia was a notoriously cruel ruler. She had arranged the murder of many enemies. She had murdered her husband. She had arranged the murder of her son. The Empress thought nothing of putting servants to death if they made a mistake. They died, without fail, by strangling, at 4 a.m., while she had breakfast.

Therefore, the Lord High Chamberlain was alarmed when the Empress commanded him to arrange a banquet in honour of the Siamese ambassador.

"Your Majesty, this is very short notice. The recent flooding has cut us off from supplies," he murmured, lying on the floor before her throne, his face pressed against the tiles.

"You must obey my commands or suffer the penalty," replied the Empress.

The Lord High Chamberlain crawled backwards for five minutes. The Imperial guards opened the throne-room doors, and he crawled backwards through them. Then he rose to his feet and hastened along vast corridors to the kitchens, where the 42 palace cooks promptly stopped whatever they were doing and fell to the floor, pressing their faces against the tiles.

For a thousand years, an imperial banquet had consisted of 190 servings. It happened that there was plenty of fish, fowl and other meat in the larders. Fruit had been dried and stored. Spices were plentiful. However, a 50-gram individual portion of rice was essential, and reserves of rice had run woefully low as a result of the floods. No more could be obtained in time.

"We have only nine-and-a-half clay jars of rice left," the chief cook reported. "Should I write my will?"

So few kilogram jars? The Lord High Chamberlain's face turned grey. In a husky voice, he said, "Yes, for we will certainly die."

Was he correct in his calculations?

1 2 3 4 5 6 7 8 9 0

Fuel Fear

"Darn it," said Mr Fung, peering at the gauge. "I've only got five litres left in the tank. In the rush, I forgot to fuel up."

Tsing was in the back of the car. He leaned over the front seat and peered at the clock on the dashboard. "But Dad, it's 2.09 p.m.," he said.

Mr Fung felt a deep pang of guilt. Tsing had turned out to be a brilliant goal-scorer for the school A-team. The team had spent months battling their way through the schools' league to the final. Kick-off for the cup match was at 3 p.m., and here he was, running out of fuel and letting the boy down.

"Don't worry, Dad," Tsing said, seeing his father's expression. This made Mr Fung feel even worse. Tsing didn't deserve this.

"How far is it to the ground, Dad?" Tsing asked.

His father checked the dials. "Twenty-five kilometres," he said.

Tsing reached into the glove-box and pulled out the car's handbook. "The car does five kilometres per litre, at an average 30 kph," he said. "We should be OK."

Yes, thought Mr Fung miserably, but if we slow to thirty to complete the twenty-five kilometres, will we get there in time?

Did they?

1234567890

Grim Gondola

Peter and Arthur worked in the same office and shared a love of skiing. They had arranged to go on a skiing holiday together and were staying at the resort of Alp de Ruez.

On their first morning in the sunshine of the mountain peaks, they rose early, put on their ski outfits, and boarded the gondola cableway that departed from the village square.

As their cabin moved away from the station, swaying gently, Peter and Arthur gazed out over the sunny white slopes, looking forward to their first outing in the fresh morning snow, with few other skiers in sight.

In a few minutes, they were nearing the station, perched on the edge of a towering cliff. Peter was adjusting the clips of his ski-boots and Arthur was scratching a speck from the polished base of one of his skis, when suddenly the cabin jerked to a halt.

Both men climbed back to their feet and peered up ahead. Peter counted aloud: five cabins dangled on their line between their cabin and the station. Beneath their cabin, three hundred metres below, a rash of jagged black rocks poked cruelly out of the snow.

Arthur pulled out his pocket radio, which he had tuned earlier to the resort's frequency, to hear the weather forecast. It was broadcasting an emergency warning in French, followed by German, then English. "This is an alert. Clear the slopes beneath the main gondola cableway within

90 seconds. A rupture has been detected in the haulage cable. We are working to restore emergency low-speed of two cabins through the station per minute, and will unload passengers at that rate. Repeat, we will unload passengers. Remain calm."

"Phew, this is going to be a nervous wait!" Arthur said, trying to appear cheerful.

Peter had turned white. "Better say your prayers, old friend," he said.

Why?

123456789 0

Gunk

The Duke of Beltingham stared at the pond that lay at the centre of his enormous park. It reflected the wide walls and towers of Beltingham Palace, which had no fewer than 48 bedrooms.

"When did you put the treatment in the pond?" he asked his groundsman, Mr Relch, who stood wringing his hands.

"Day before yesterday, your grace," the groundsman mumbled. "It were s'posed to kill them weeds."

Both men stared at the layer of green slime which covered one-quarter of the surface of the water.

"So you called the factory and they said it must be past its sell-by date?"

"Ay, your grace," the groundsman replied. "Them said yon layer of guck'd double in size every day."

"Hmmm," the duke rubbed his chin. "If it gets to cover the whole pond, every precious carp and pike I own will die right away. You say they're sending a bottle of remedy over?"

"Indeed they are, your grace. Parcel post. Be here in three days."

The duke perked up, and twisted his moustache. "That's very good, Retch. See to it you apply the remedy promptly, and you'll keep your job, instead of being fired."

Retch watched the duke turn away and stride back towards Beltingham Palace. He scratched his head and groaned, wondering how he'd ever find another job.

Why?

1 2 3 4 5 6 7 8 9 0

Handy Andy

Andy's friends knew he was bright. He learned all the cheats for his computer games on day one, when the game came out. He traded his games in about a week after he got them, when most other people were still at the training-mode stage.

He'd sit there in his room, leaning his head on his right hand as he wrote down the answers to his homework, and he practically never made a mistake.

His brother, Rick, was visiting his friend Greg one night. Greg had been given a new joystick. It was bigger and better than any joystick anybody had seen before. It had more buttons than any other model ever made. They were dotted all over the left side of the handle, so you wrapped your fingers round and played them like a piano keyboard. Shoot. Stop. Freeze. Repeat. Replay . . . so many functions you thought you'd never remember them all.

The boys played this new game Rick brought along. It was a super-intelligent 3-D action game called *Mongolian Rage*. Nobody got past training mode that night. They photocopied the instruction book on Greg's dad's copier and took it home to study.

Next night they got together again and played *Mongolian Rage* some more. Nobody scored very highly.

"Hey," said Greg, "we have to get Andy over to master this game. I'll bet he could score the max before the end of one session like this."

"No one would lay odds on that," somebody said.

"I would," Rick said quietly.

They all looked at him.

"You'd lay odds against your brother? Your super-smart brother?" Greg said incredulously.

"Fifty-to-one he scores no better than any of us did tonight."

"Fifty-to-one?" Greg was already reaching into his pocket. "Here's one says you're wrong. You're going to be paying me fifty tomorrow night. Now, what shall I buy with that?"

Greg started chatting busily with everyone about what he was going to get with Rick's money when Andy cracked *Mongolian Rage* and scored max in about a half-hour.

Rick simply laid his money against Greg's and looked forward to tomorrow night.

Why was Rick so confident?

1 2 3 4 5 6 7 8 9 0

A Heroic Moment

The people of Peranga, in the Andes, were starved and out of work. The rich were as fat as their Swiss bank accounts. Only one man was brave enough to face the fat ones and the brutal police. He was Don Bravado, with the enormous black moustache.

Don Bravado rode down with his men into the valleys, burned ranches, rustled cattle, plundered gold, and gave it all to the poor. Then he rode back into the mountains, where he sang songs at the fireside, stroked his whiskers, and told stories of how he would free the people.

Everybody loved Don Bravado, except the rich. They wanted his corpse on a plank, and El Tornado had sworn to deliver it. Having been appointed the president's chief of security, El Tornado rode into the mountains. He hunted Don Bravado down, lassooed him, and dragged him away. It took six hours to get to the compound. There, a fat judge condemned thin Don Bravado to death.

The firing squad gathered at dawn. Don Bravado stood to attention. He had a pistol concealed up his sleeve. He stared at the three soldiers with rifles trained on his heart. They were men of iron discipline, who would only fire when given the word.

"I will count one-alligator, two-alligators, three-alligators," said El Tornado. He chuckled. "Then you die."

Don Bravado smiled. He knew from experience that it would take him one second to aim and shoot at each man. Then he could run for the hills. He whipped out his gun and started to fire.

Did Don Bravado survive?

1 2 3 4 5 6 7 8 9 0

Jumbo Terror

The world's single most planet-wrecking vehicle, the *Cordiale*, soared 20 kilometres above the Atlantic, spewing pollution into the ozone layer and hurrying eight crew and 160 rich people to New York and the next day of their pampered, luxurious lives.

"It was great in Paris, but I have definitely eaten something funny," Edwina Steinburger told her husband, Lorne Steinburger the Third, in row 3.

In row 9, Binky the supermodel told the steward, "I feel so bad I think I'm going to bring it all up."

In row 14, one of the richest pop singers who ever lived buckled forward with his pulse slowing.

The air crew line jangled in the cockpit. The second officer took the message and turned pale. The captain snapped, "What is it?"

"Suspected food poisoning in the cabin, sir. Must have been the oysters."

Without hesitation, the captain cut in on the call. "Exactly when were the oysters served?"

The air crew chief came back almost as promptly. "We finished serving them 20 minutes ago. They took only a few minutes to distribute and everybody loved them, including us."

"How many cases so far?" the captain snapped.

"Forty, sir. One of them fatal." The captain and his second officer exchanged glances. They, too, had snacked on the oysters.

The captain tapped a gauge, and examined the computer numbers on it – one hour and forty-three minutes exactly to landing at JFK airport. Without hesitation, he pressed the Mayday emergency button.

Why?

Lancelot

Sir Lancelot had the power to see blue dragons – a special gift he had won in combat. He had five such dragons lying captured in his dungeons, gradually losing their strength.

The Lady of the Lake controlled the blue dragons. She had unleashed all seven of them against the remote mountain castle of Sir Lancelot. He had rejected her love. Now he must be driven into exile.

Sir Lancelot patrolled on his white charger through a landscape dotted with spiky grey trees, a flaming red sunset lighting up the sky behind him.

Suddenly, from behind a jagged crag of scarlet rock, two massive blue dragons leapt out, blocking the sun. The stinking smoke belching from their nostrils made the sky dark, as if night had fallen. Sir Lancelot's special vision no longer worked. He was blinded.

"You are surrounded!" thundered dragon voices. They were so loud, Sir Lancelot's armour rattled. "Surrender now! Our Lady has promised you mercy. You will only be transported 50 light years to another galaxy!"

Sir Lancelot chuckled quietly, opened the handle of his sword, and pressed a hidden button there.

Why was he so confident?

1 2 3 4 5 6 7 8 9 0

Last Goodbye

In his luxury private jet, flying at 10,000 metres towards England, Prince Mustafa Osman was having a spot of bother. Seated in his golden bathtub, he was staring at Ahmed, his chief of staff, who had just informed him that the prince's pilot had suffered a fatal heart attack. Prince Mustafa inquired, "Who, then, is flying the plane?"

"Nobody, your excellency," the chief of staff replied.

"Then take charge," the prince snapped. "I am in my bath."

After pulling the dead pilot out of his seat and dropping him on the cockpit floor, Ahmed blankly surveyed the controls. There were hundreds of dials, knobs, switches, levers, toggles, handles, keys and buttons. Through the windscreen was the side of a mountain, approaching fast. Ahmed thought of Natasha, awaiting him in the VIP lounge at London Heathrow airport. He eyed the pilot's radio-telephone unit, and felt just the slightest twinge of alarm. A final call to the love of his life, explaining his predicament, assuring her of his eternal passion, and giving her the code of his safe, would take at least two minutes.

The Prince's colossally expensive jet was going to crash into a wall of rock in . . . Ahmed examined the speedometer. "600 kilometres per hour." He peered at the radar screen. "Ah good, the precipice is a kilometre away."

In a spurt of activity, he pulled out his personal organizer and keyed in Natasha's name. Her mobile phone number appeared.

Did Ahmed have time for the call?

1234567890

Moon Ladder

Grenjo Esti addressed his people on the third day of winter, 2065. He spoke to them as follows:

"The opposing forces have been smashed. They have all been exterminated. But the cost has been high. War broke out in 2000. We have been at war for 65 years. Nothing has been made since the war started. We used all the 500 million vehicles then in existence to fight with. They are all we have left, but there is no fuel for them. All farming has been destroyed. The seven continents lie in poisoned ruins.

"Only one good thing has happened in 65 years of war. We no longer need air to breathe because cosmic rays feed our blood and bone marrow. We no longer need to eat, because solar rays sustain our energy. The war has destroyed planet Earth. Only the life pods we built on the moon remain of any use to us. It is time to leave Earth and go to the moon. Follow me!"

The people raged and shouted at Grenjo Esti. They did not want to leave their home planet. A rival leader, Rongbeg Rignold, leapt on to an overturned lorry and yelled to the vast crowd:

"How can we go to the moon? All aviation and rocketry was destroyed in 2000. We will perish here on Earth. The solar system will be well rid of us. Perhaps without us, life will, one day, be reborn on Earth."

Grenjo Esti signalled for quiet. The people fell silent.

Grenjo stared bravely over the sea of watching faces. What could he say? As a general, he had always used the same speech: " Attack! Kill! Plunder! Follow me!" It had always worked for him. Now he had blurted the first thing that came into his head. How could he follow it up, and stop that cowardly worm Rongbeg Rignold taking over?

Grenjo gazed up into the slowly burning atmosphere far overhead. Inspiration came to him. He made a quick calculation. Then he spoke:

"We will collect the entire vehicle fleet. Each vehicle is at least two metres high. We will stack them on top of each other until they reach the moon's average distance from Earth*. We will wait until the moon passes within reach of the stack, and we will climb up it and leave this doomed planet."

The people scratched their heads in wonder. Wise men crouched in circles and drew numbers in the scorched sand.

Did Grenjo remain leader of the human race?

*The moon's average distance from Earth is 384,400 kilometres

Nuclear Nightmare

Dick Widgett, chief engineer, clenched his fists in despair and stared up at the matrix mimic board, which showed, in clever red filaments of electric light, the scheme of his nuclear power plant. The plant he had designed. The plant he had built. The plant he had run for five years. The plant which was now threatening to go critical and blow up, taking with it the nearby city, and the lives of a million people.

In the space of a sweating, cursing, ranting, frantic half-hour, Dick Widgett, the legend, the benefactor of the human race, the Nobel prize candidate, had turned into that wretch Widgett, the incompetent monster who single-handedly threatened to destroy a technical dream by causing the single biggest disaster in human history.

Until five minutes ago, his dozens of assistants, men and women in white coats and spectacles, who carried clipboards in their hands and strings of scientific qualifications after their names, had been running round at his command. Now, they had been evacuated.

Only Dick Widgett remained, staring up at the matrix mimic board and the digital read-out, which counted down the seconds in red numbers. Sixty-three seconds. Sixty-two. Sixty-one.

Widgett knew that if he switched Control Rod Drives 1 and 2 into reverse, the plant would never function again. He had designed it that way, believing this accident could never happen. If he left them in place, the reactors would go critical and melt down. The trouble was, he had switched Drive 2 into reverse – he glanced at a dial – three minutes and forty-five seconds ago. Drives took four minutes to withdraw their control rods and shut down nuclear reaction. Drive 1 he had switched – he checked another gauge – two minutes and forty-five seconds ago.

With the back of a trembling hand, he stopped trickles of sweat running down his brow into his eyes.

"I have three doctorates and two master degrees, and I am too panicked to figure out whether I should get out of here or not," he muttered, rooted to the spot.

Did Dick Widgett's disaster occur?

1 2 3 4 5 6 7 8 9 0

Pacific Panic

The five-masted sailing ship, *Queen Catherine*, was under full sail in favourable conditions in the South Pacific Ocean on 18 July, 1802, when she hit very sudden typhoon conditions. It was three o'clock in the morning and totally dark.

The navigator awakened Captain Stollard in his cabin. Without warning, the wind was gusting at over 100 kilometres per hour. Waves were reaching a mountainous 10 metres. The skipper rose without a word, and hurried to the bridge. He stared out at the rigging in mounting alarm. In the light from the cabin, every sheet and line supporting the 28 spread sails could be seen stretched taut to breaking point. The howling gale hitting the massive sail was driving the prow of his ship into the towering waves with shattering force, making the vessel's frame shudder. His magnificent ship, the pride of the British merchant navy, was in danger of plunging straight to the bottom of the sea with the loss of 185 hands and a cargo worth millions of pounds.

Could he reef the sails in time to save the ship? Or should he take the enormous risk of heaving to, turning towards the wind, and possibly destroying the ship's masts or even cause her to founder? It took six hands aloft to reef a sail. He scratched his chin, trying to clear the sleep from his brain. He had to be sure there were enough hands on board to reef the sails, without leaving the ship otherwise unmanned.

What did he decide?

1 2 3 4 5 6 7 8 9 0

Penalty

Rudi Sinatra, home-team goalie, waited between the goalposts. This was the climax of watching hundreds of videos of Greg Shah shooting penalties.

Greg Shah, highest-paid striker on earth, placed the black and white football on the field and took four paces backwards.

The news team held their cameras.

The crowd of 89,000 held their breath.

Boot met ball with a thump. Rudi dived right, the ball went right. He caught it.

The stadium went wild.

Minutes later, another foul by the home team. Greg took a couple of paces back, his boot met the ball. Rudi dived left, saved the goal.

The crowd went mad.

Another penalty quickly followed. Greg Shah took four paces backwards. Boot met ball. Rudi dived right, saved the goal.

The crowd went wild.

This was the TV Globe cup. Five hundred million fans watched out there. For most of the second half, it remained three goals to three. In injury time, there was a home-team foul. The crowd gasped in horror. A dreadful silence fell.

Greg Shah bent to place the ball the way he liked it. He stood up, stepped back three paces and took aim. Boot met ball. Rudi leaped up in the air, snatched the ball from under the crossbar. The crowd went mad.

Penalty shoot-out time. Their goalie was inspired, but after three shots, he let one in.

It all hung on Rudi now. If he saved this one, his name would go down in history.

Greg Shah placed the ball, took four paces back.

The cameras zoomed in on Rudi. His face was composed. He looked totally confident.

Why?

1234567890

Perisc-Hope

Able Seaman Abel Siemens took a fresh grip on the handles either side of the *Arethusa*'s periscope with palms that were slippery with sweat. He peered hard into the lenses, remembering the prayer that his mother, Inaida Siemens, had taught him to say if he was ever in deadly danger. Framed in the viewfinder was the stark shape of the enemy battleship, outlined on the horizon against the rising sun.

The reassuring voice of the skipper, Commander Mander, was crisp and clear in Abel's headset: "The enemy's depth-charger can cripple us as far as 150 metres under water. His radar will detect us in exactly two minutes. We dive at one point five metres per second."

As the command followed immediately: "Dive!", Abel retracted the periscope and breathed a sigh of relief.

Why?

1 2 3 4 5 6 7 8 9 0

Rajah's Temples

The rajah of Jellyrich turned to the enormous window of his castle. He looked out over the perfectly landscaped park. High white walls enclosed a vast space. Against the near wall could be seen a large ornamental lake. A field of grass lay between this stretch of water and another lake. Altogether there were seven lakes, the last lying against a white wall far away in the hazy distance.

The rajah glanced away to the east, and growled. There, rising serene and beautiful, was the temple built by his neighbour.

"This building makes me look foolish," the rajah said to his chancellor, who was kneeling behind him. "See, here come my seven daughters in seven coaches. They are the seven most beautiful women in all India. In just a few minutes, when they have assembled here, I will announce that a temple more beautiful than that of my neighbour shall be built for each of them. I have seven lakes, and a temple will be built on each grassy field that lies between them. Seven lofty temples! Then see who looks a fool, I or my neighbour."

The rajah turned triumphantly to face his chancellor. When he met the chancellor's gaze, it was troubled. The rajah frowned.

"What is this? Do you question the will of your lord and master?"

"Never, esteemed one, but I am afraid your plan is impossible," the chancellor replied.

Why did the chancellor risk his life with such a reply?

Rodent Relief

Jane and Peter had a packet of 13 biscuits for a picnic, and were exploring the cellar. A draught slammed the door behind them. The outside latch fell. They were trapped.

A large, mean-looking rat emerged from a hole. Eyeing them nastily, it moved towards the children. Jane threw one of her biscuits at it. Checking the face of her new digital watch, she noted that the rat took 15 seconds to hungrily devour the biscuit, while Peter frantically got out his mobile phone. The firefighters told him they would rush over in exactly three minutes.

"No problem," said Jane.

How could she stay so cool?

Short Cuts

Terry Blades faced the board of directors of GAYMESCORP.
They were seated at the three-tonne gold-plated table on the
seventy-second floor of the GAYM Tower in Tokyo, the
world's fifth-tallest building.

Pranque, the biggest-selling game in history, had been
launched nine months earlier. Using new laser-quantum
technology, it had offered graphics more real than the naked
eye could see, sounds more acute than the naked ear could
hear, and special effects faster than the brain could
comprehend. By Christmas it had sold more than 900
million units, netting GAYMESCORP a sudden one billion
dollars in profit.

Before it earned a billion, hackers had immediately tried to crack *Pranque*'s short cuts. However, they had collided with Terry's brilliantly clever software code. Nobody had ever seen a defence system like it. It took the world's cleverest hackers three months to reveal the first short cut, one that doubled a champion player's speed. After that, to the amazement of the trade – nothing. But two weeks ago, just one similar short cut had been discovered.

Mr Fuji Hawa, president of GAYMESCORP, rose and went to a large reinforced metal door. He operated three coded locks, and company staff pulled the heavy door open. Inside was an enormous, brightly lit library. It had stacks of shelves that stretched away into the distance. On them were ranged an incredible number of CD and DVD packs. Terry gasped. There was only one thing that this astonishing array of games could be. It was the secret collection – thousands and thousands of superb, top-flight games, designed by the most brilliant minds in the world.

GAYMESCORP had used its huge profits to buy them up and hide them away. It was a sure-fire way to send *Pranque* soaring to the top of the charts. *Pranque*'s creator had bought up practically all the other good games on Earth.

"Your protective software fought off the *Pranque* hackers," Mister Fuki Hawa said. "I am offering you a special choice as a bonus for your work. The world champion *Pranque* player is here. You can take one hundred thousand dollars, or you can take whatever you like from the special collection for as long as the champion's *Pranque* game lasts. His original world record was one hour, four minutes and eight seconds. Which do you choose?"

Terry gazed at the shelves of superb, unknown games. He yearned to wander along the shelves, looking at all the titles and the authors, many of which he would know. He thought of the stacks of priceless games he could carry away.

"I'll take the hundred thousand," he said.

Why?

1 2 3 4 5 6 7 8 9 0

Siege Headache

Sir Rudyard stood before his enormous fireplace in the keep, a huge 2-metre tall figure, wearing all his stiff armour, save the helmet, which lay on the table. Through the windows, men were hurrying to and fro across the courtyard, carrying pails of water, bundles of arrows and baskets of bolts. Along the battlements that surrounded the courtyard, hundreds of soldiers were firing crossbows, shooting arrows and tipping boiling oil onto the enemy. The sky was streaked with smoke from the many fires in the castle roofs, and there was a constant hubbub of shouting, screaming and groaning.

"Sire, I beg you, make use of the tunnel," urged Gandalf, Sir Rudyard's steward, who had squeezed his little wife into the 1-metre high escape route only an hour earlier. "The bolts are running out, and we are down to a hundred arrows. The enemy has placed twenty ladders against the walls, and soon his men will be streaming over the battlements."

The knight heaved a deep sigh. "We need 500 arrows for an hour's battle, and easily 100 men per hour can climb each ladder. I can't do the sum. Perhaps we will be able to hold them off. Certainly, I shall not be using the tunnel."

What calculation did the knight make that persuaded him to fight on, instead of using the tunnel to escape?

$1\ 2\ 3\ 4\ 5\ 6\ 7\ 8\ 9\ 0$

Space Battle Command

He is Solar Overlord ZAKLAR, a tall, third-generation cyborg controlled by on-board human gene banks. His warriors worship him as a god.

His campaign to win this solar system's greatest treasure, the green planet YALWA, now only 100,000 kilometres away, has lasted 30 years. Upon its shores, his love, the beautiful KLARRA, longingly awaits him.

Suddenly Central Navigator Module's auto-voice rings out, "Emergency! Emergency! Entering asteroid belt in four-point-three seconds."

ZAKLAR glances at his bio-radar wall. It reads his mind and replies, "101 of your starships remain battle-ready, Overlord! You have lost 1000 over the last million kilometres."

It's now or never. All battle systems go automatic in the asteroids. The decision is ZAKLAR'S. He has the measure of enemy power. He needs only one battle starship to rescue KLARRA and escape down a time-warp.

Two command controls flash up:

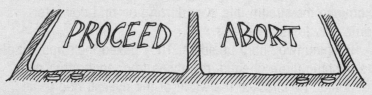

Which does he press?

Stony Steps

Curtis ran through the woods at top speed, ducking to avoid branches, and weaving to dodge dead twigs that might crack under his feet.

He paused for a second to listen. Over the beating of his heart and the gasping of his breath he could hear the others not far behind, crashing and shouting to each other. They had no reason to be silent. He was the quarry, not they. As he listened, he became aware of unexpected sounds ahead. He crept forward to a boulder, climbed over it and stared down in dismay. The woods were deeply divided by a rocky crevasse, which had been cut by a plunging mountain stream. He considered his way down the side. He could pick his way down the rocks to a gravel beach at the edge of the stream, but the water was too fast and deep to wade across or to swim.

He glanced behind him. The snapping branches and crunching twigs, the urgent cries, were fast approaching. There was no turning back, and the hunters were spread out too far for him to escape to right or left. He turned and examined the stream, his eyes darting up and down for some way to save himself.

He spied two sharp boulders. They poked their tips out of the dashing foam at equal distances from each other and the banks. He checked the width of the river. It had to be eight metres wide. He knew he could jump two metres if he

really tried. Right! No problem!
	He climbed over the rocks and down into the ravine.

Did he get away?

1 2 3 4 5 6 7 8 9 0

Tennis Tension

The world championships were the climactic point of
Bennie's life, and a historic first in the game. He'd started
the season with nothing. Now, his fiancée, the Hollywood
star Lynda Layne, was in the audience, sitting beside his
mother and father. His trainer was watching, along with
450 million television viewers. Among them were his
sponsors, Hi-Line Trainers, who had paid four million
dollars for him to wear their label on his shirt. He was
playing with a Randall Rose racket, which Mr Rose had paid
another four million dollars for Bennie to use. And on his
cap, he was wearing the symbol of the Gordian tennis ball
company, which had paid two million for the privilege.

When he won the world championship (not "if" he won –
you just did not think about not winning) he would receive
another ten million dollars by contract. If he did not win
then the consequences were too horrible to imagine. He
knew all the bright lights would go out, Lynda would take
that acting part they had offered her in Africa, and the tax
man had promised to crack down on that four million dollar
tax bill.

The trouble was, it was scorching hot, and his opponent
was on top form. They were even sets, and Bennie was
serving to decide the tie-breaker.

His first serve packed the usual punch, but it went wide.
"Out," called the line judge.

His second serve was almost as powerful, and curved beautifully down the service line. It looked so good, Bennie's heart leapt. His opponent could never return it.

"Out," called the line judge.

Bennie went into a fog. The crowd roared as his opponent vaulted the net. Tears filled his eyes, and he lost track of time.

Things only became real again when he found Lynda staring into his eyes.

"Don't worry, darling, you'll still be worth sixteen million bucks when this is all over."

Bennie forced a smile that was half a frown.

Was Lynda right?

1 2 3 4 5 6 7 8 9 0

Track Terror

Fred Devere had never worked a day in his life, apart from betting on horses. He went to the track almost every day, and bet on almost every race. Like many full-time gamblers, he was superstitious. Any sign was enough to influence his betting decision.

One windy day in early March, when the tracks were drying off nicely for some fine flat-racing in the season, the worst shock of his career occurred. Here's how it happened:

He noticed, upon picking up his morning copy of the Racing Times, that it was the seventh of the month, and that the numbers of the year, 1992, added up to a number divisible by seven. When, prompted by this discovery, he looked up the seventh race at Haydock Park racetrack, he found that both names of the horse he liked, Garry Glade, started with the seventh letter of the alphabet. Furthermore, the names of its trainer, Grahame Goodman, also began with that letter, and both his names consisted of seven letters.

At the railway station, he noted in passing that his train departed at 11.37 from platform 7. At the track, he was required to enter by none other than gate seven. To his astonishment, the odds on Garry Glade to win were seven-to-one.

When he reached the betting counter, Fred was so

excited that he splashed out £7,000 on Garry Glade's victory.

How much did he earn?

1 2 3 4 5 6 7 8 9 0

Truck Crazy

Gregg drove his three-way tipper truck west at top speed. The 185-horsepower engine hummed happily, as though it had not noticed the seven-tonne load of earth that had been heaped onto the loading platform behind the driver's cab.

"It's a horrible night," Gregg thought, dreaming of being home with Kathy, his wife, and watching a comedy video by the gas fire.

Rain lashed the bodywork of the truck. The wipers worked at full speed. The voice on the radio warned of worse to come. Straight ahead, the sun was like a fried egg, sinking below the horizon.

Darkness fell. Gregg switched on his lights and picked out the sign which showed his side road, the one which led to the farm where he had to dump the truck's load.

He felt like getting out his mobile phone and calling Kathy. He could ask her to walk up and rent that new film from the video library and to pick up some chocolate while she's there.

He never saw where the dog came from. It just appeared in his headlights, streaked with rain, a black-and-white sheepdog, with eyes that shone red. The braking worked, he avoided the dog, but the wheels locked from the heavy load, and his tyres started to aquaplane – skidding over the surface of the water, failing to get a grip on the road.

Gregg saw the sharp corner ahead, reckoning that it was approximately 100 metres away. His speedometer said 90 kph – yes, he'd been daydreaming – and he did a rapid calculation: either he jumped out of the cab and wrecked his lorry, or he held on.

Which did he decide to do?

Water Shortage

Water was becoming very scarce in the land of Samsara by 2020. In the summer of 2023, the rivers ran dry. Tankers of water had to be ordered in from neighbouring countries. The government imposed rationing. Normal daily usage of 170 litres per meter was slashed to 11 litres. There were severe fines for people found using more than that when their water meters were inspected.

Naïm (pronounced Nay-eem) lived in a little town in Samsara. He was seven years old and very helpful to his mother, a widow who lived in a little upstairs flat, just off the main street. Naïm ran errands, helped with the housekeeping, and changed the channels on the television. With all this responsibility, he had also learned to think about the family accounts.

Passing frequently by the river that ran through the town, he had noticed its waters declining. He was not surprised when water rationing was announced. But it was easy to forget. After putting two bricks into the toilet cistern, sealing half the holes in the showerhead and giving the mains tap a turn to reduce water pressure, he gave the matter little more thought.

Then his friend from the flat downstairs came to the door to warn him that the water inspector was looking at the meters in the entrance hall. Suddenly, Naïm was worried – his mother could face a crippling fine if they had used too much water. He ran through a day's use in his head. One flush: three litres. One basin of water: four litres. One half-minute shower: three litres. One toothbrushing: one litre. Phew! That should be all right.

The doorbell rang. Naïm went and opened it. A big man in a uniform stood there. His badge said: Water Board Inspector. Naïm smiled, but he was in for a shock.

Why?

Answers

Almost a Million

No. For one thing, Gerald started off with the wrong calculation – one minute and 26.4 seconds is not the same as 1.264 minutes. Anyway, it took him several minutes to do the calculation on paper. But his biggest mistake was that he failed to notice that the robot message told him @500 was noon. Therefore, @499 was one minute and 26.4 seconds before noon. He had about one minute to send his "sell" message to the stockbroker.

A Big Pile of Computer Games

Fangio quickly worked out that from June 6 to August 31 there are only 87 days, not 88. There are 62 days in July and August and 25 days left of June. 62 + 25 = 87. He would never have received any games from his wily dad.

Block Head

The complex consisted of 36 laboratories arranged in a square on a grid of streets. The complex was, therefore, six buildings square. The main street bisected the square, which meant there were three blocks on either side of it. It was not possible to turn right and go five blocks west so Blond knew the instructions were false – there was no meeting, and the Doctor had other plans for him (evidently villainous ones, since he had lied).

Brave Knight

The king appeared to make a sporting gesture by choosing a shorter horse than that ridden by Lord Randall. In fact, whilst sitting in the saddle, he was 15 cm taller than Lord Randall, so even on a horse 10 cm shorter, he would still be 5 cm taller than the lord. This would place the king's lance five deciding centimetres higher.

Cake

Dimple Ray ate one cake, his challenger ate three. "Most cakes" was the challenge, so Dimple Ray lost.

Compass Conundrum

One of the worst oil disasters in history. All the captain needed to remember was that his vessel could not halt in less than five kilometres. The Mexican coast was four kilometres away. A collision was unavoidable.

Crag-Hanger

Naomi only managed to connect by one hand (four fingers). Tara started to pray because she was already falling through the air.

Desert Dilemma

One litre can keep a camel going for one hour, so on 200 litres a camel could survive for 200 hours. There are 24 hours in a day, so 200 hours is 8.3 days (200 ÷ 24). Ahmed's goal was seven days away, and he could reach it with a day's camel-power to spare.

Detective Doubt

No, all three women had alibis, and Ruggles chose one of

them. One man, the gardener, also had an alibi. Only the boy did not.

Disc Dilemma
If the discs were not laid flat in a stack of 1,800, but balanced on end, the 12cm diameter CDs would stack only 15 high.

DJ Sonic
The four tracks can be played in 16 different orders, and each song lasts for 2 minutes. The CD will last for 8 minutes each time it is played (4 songs x 2 minutes). If the tracks on the CD are played in sixteen different orders, then total playing time amounts to 128 minutes (16 x 8). DJ Sonic's radio show goes off the air at midnight, in 32 minutes, so by the time the last sequence ends, the show will have been off the air for over an hour and a half.

Electro-Detector
Jamie's dad got a stiff fine for exceeding 2,000 watts consumption. Jamie and his babysitter forgot why his bedroom was warm and cosy on a chilly night. Each room had a 750W individual electric heater that needed turning on and off. They forgot to turn it off, and the house was using about 610 watts too much power.

Expedition
Keeping the sharp end of the piece of cake facing him, the Professor pointed one straight side of the piece of cake at the sun rising in the east. The other straight side, pointing left at 90 degrees, showed his route northwards.

Farran's Frightener

Sultan pointed out that only six dozen (6 x 12) or 72 apple danish had been made. Four remained in the shop, so (72 - 4) 68 must have been sold. The fatal dose for one person was 3 apple danishes, so for thirty-six people to die (36 x 3) 108 tainted apple danishes would have had to be eaten, far more than the number sold in Farran's bakery. The forensic laboratory must have made an error.

Fatal Food

No, because in their panicking, officials must have made a mistake in their mental arithmetic. Nine-and-a-half jars filled with a kilogram of rice each provided (9.5 x 1000) 9500 grams of rice. The banquet required 190 50-gram portions (190 x 50), which makes 9500 grams of rice. There was exactly enough to go round.

Fuel Fear

They made it. At 30kph, Mr Fung's car was doing (30 kilometres per hour ÷ 60 minutes in an hour) 0.5 kilometres per minute, or one kilometre every two minutes. Twenty-five kilometres would therefore take (25 kilometres x 2 minutes) 50 minutes. The time is 2.09p.m., 51 minutes before the kick-off, leaving (51 minutes to kick off - 50 minutes before arrival) 1 minute to spare.

Grim Gondola

The authorities expected disaster within one-and-a-half minutes. In that time, three cabins could pass through the station and unload. Peter and Arthur's sixth cabin was doomed to fall hundreds of metres onto jagged rocks.

Gunk

The gunk would double to cover half the pond next day, and double to cover the pond the day after. The remedy would not arrive until the day after that, by which time the duke's fish would be dead.

Handy Andy

Rick knew Andy was left-handed (he leant on his right hand and wrote with his left whilst doing his homework), and a joystick designed specially for right-handed people would be no good to him. Rick won fifty from Greg the next evening.

A Heroic Moment

El Tornado counted to three while Don Bravado brought down the firing squad. But Don Bravado failed to take into account the fact that El Tornado also had a gun. He did not survive.

Jumbo Terror

Passengers were falling seriously ill or dying at a rate 2 per minute (20 minutes ÷ 40 casualties). Therefore, all 168 persons aboard could be expected to go down within 84 minutes (168 people ÷ 2 casualties per minute). The aeroplane is one hour and forty-three minutes away from landing, that is 103 minutes, so all persons on board can be expected to be taken ill 19 minutes before landing (103 - 84).

Lancelot

Sir Lancelot had five of the Lady of the Lake's dragons locked away. He could not be surrounded as the two he had seen in front of him, to the west, were the only ones she had left from the original seven.

Last Goodbye

Alas! The Prince's jet was travelling towards the cliff at 10 kilometres per minute (600 km per hour ÷ 60 minutes in an hour). It would hit the cliff (one km away) within one-tenth of a minute, or six seconds – barely time to key in Natasha's number on the radio phone.

Moon Ladder

Answer: Yes. Grenjo easily worked out that 500 million vehicles with an average height of two metres would stack 1,000 million metres, or 1 million kilometres – far further than needed to reach the moon.

Nuclear Nightmare

With 60 seconds to go, Drive 2 would withdraw in 15 seconds. Drive 1, however, would take another one minute and 15 seconds before meltdown, bringing catastrophe.

Pacific Panic

He reefed. Each sail required 6 hands to reef, so to reef 28 sails required (6 x 28) 168 hands, leaving the captain with (185 - 168) 17 of the 185 hands on board to help on deck.

Penalty

Rudi had studied Greg's technique – two paces back meant he would shoot to the left, three paces back meant he aimed the ball for the centre, and four paces back, for this deciding penalty, meant that the ball would go right. Rudi knew he could save it, and he did.

Perisc-Hope

Abel knew the *Arethusa* would dive to a safe depth of 150

metres within 100 seconds, giving the sub 20 seconds to spare.

Rajah's Temples
Between the seven lakes there were only six fields, so only six temples could be built.

Rodent Relief
Jane knew that if the rat could eat one biscuit in 15 seconds, then 12 biscuits would take the rat at least 180 seconds (15 x 12), or 3 minutes, to eat, by which time the firefighters would have arrived.

Shortcuts
Mister Hawa was merely showing off his collection. The discovery of *Pranque*'s second short cut had ruined its value. The first short cut had doubled a champion's speed, cutting the game to just over half an hour, but the second short cut had doubled the player's speed again, meaning *Pranque* could be beaten in just a few moments. Terry Blades knew he would only have had time to grab a few CDs from the shelves.

Siege Headache
Sir Rudyard stood 2 metres tall and could not fit into the 1-metre high tunnel because his stiff armour didn't allow him to bend down or crawl through it.

Space Battle Command
Zaklar calculates that he has lost one battle starship per thousand miles (1,000,000 miles ÷ 1,000 starships = 1 per 1,000). He therefore stands to lose 100 starships over

the next 100,000 miles, leaving one starship intact, which is hopefully his own. He presses Proceed.

Stony Steps
The two stepping stones were evenly spaced across eight metres, dividing the distance into three jumps of 2m 60cm each ($8 \div 3 = 2.6$). Curtis did not make it across the river.

Tennis Tension
No. Bennie's payments totalled $10 million. The tax department would remove $4 million, leaving him with only $6 million.

Track Terror
Nothing. Garry Glade came in seventh.

Truck Crazy
At 90 kph, Gregg was doing (90×1000) 90,000 metres per hour, or ($90,000 \div 60$)1500 metres per minute, or ($1500 \div 60$) 25 metres per second. That meant he would arrive at the corner in ($100 \div 25$) 4 seconds at his current speed. Since he was aquaplaning, he could not expect to slow down much in such a short time, so he jumped.

Water Shortage
Nam added his numbers up correctly: his consumption added up to exactly 11 litres. Unfortunately, he forgot his mother's consumption, which doubled the amount of water used in the household. Luckily, it was early days and they were let off with a small fine.

A selected list of titles available from Macmillan and Pan Books

The prices shown below are correct at the time of going to press. However, Macmillan Publishers reserve the right to show new retail prices on covers which may differ from those previously advertised.

All Macmillan titles can be ordered at your local bookshop or are available by post from:

**Book Service by Post
PO Box 29, Douglas, Isle of Man IM99 1BQ**

Credit cards accepted. For details:
Telephone: 01624 675137
Fax: 01624 670923
E-mail: bookshop@enterprise.net

Free postage and packing in the UK.
Overseas customers: add £1 per book (paperback)
and £3 per book (hardback).